About the Author

Bhavesh Praveen is a stoic. He lives with his past, taking the freeloader and the confined space with him wherever he goes. This is why he's always tired and doesn't like to visit. The tank of his replenishing morning poise is a sieve, thanks to bad experiences, the good intentions of helpful friends, and a very opinionated family. This is why he lives with his past, as he knows it and it, him. This is him trying to get it to pay rent.

A Ruby-Tooth from an Unlikely Pomegranate

Bhavesh Praveen

A Ruby-Tooth from an Unlikely Pomegranate

Olympia Publishers
London

www.olympiapublishers.com
OLYMPIA PAPERBACK EDITION

Copyright © Bhavesh Praveen 2024

The right of Bhavesh Praveen to be identified as author of
this work has been asserted in accordance with sections 77 and 78 of
the Copyright, Designs and Patents Act 1988.

All Rights Reserved

No reproduction, copy or transmission of this publication
may be made without written permission.
No paragraph of this publication may be reproduced,
copied or transmitted save with the written permission of the publisher,
or in accordance with the provisions
of the Copyright Act 1956 (as amended).

Any person who commits any unauthorised act in relation to
this publication may be liable to criminal
prosecution and civil claims for damage.

A CIP catalogue record for this title is
available from the British Library.

ISBN: 978-1-80439-542-4

This is a work of fiction.
Names, characters, places and incidents originate from the writer's
imagination. Any resemblance to actual persons, living or dead, is
purely coincidental.

First Published in 2024

Olympia Publishers
Tallis House
2 Tallis Street
London
EC4Y 0AB

Printed in Great Britain

Dedication

To my dearest Bhama, my Puuch, my muse, also my voice of reason; my degree in Mechanical Engineering, which made me rethink everything; my doubting family, for the resistance that caused the push, and my oldest friend Anju, for being there whenever it gets too crazy. I couldn't have pulled it off without you.

Acknowledgements

I thank you, dear reader, gracious motivator and confidant. I wish I could shake your hand, take in your thoughts on the book you hold, and tell you personally how eternally grateful I am for your curiosity. I am thankful to the masters: H.P. Lovecraft, for introducing me to cosmic horror; to Herman Hesse for my first taste of philosophical fiction, and the immortal Ronnie James Dio for the "Go, my son, and rock" whenever I was in dire need of it. I am grateful for Bhama, for if not for her, everything would be left to the mercy of my shockingly poor, impulsive choices. The dream of my success is shared between the two of us. I'm glad I have you, and I love you madly. Speaking of our dreams, I am grateful to Olympia for granting our most coveted wish of me becoming a published writer. I would like to thank my mother, who has been with me every step of the way from the closest point her professional life would allow. Mom, I know we have never fully understood one another—and that's okay. Thank you for your unconditional love and years of effort. I want to thank Anju, Anjana, my oldest friend—for it was her who bought me a pencil set and some charcoal while I had just buried my art dreams. Luckily there was enough air in the coffin when I dug it back out. I am grateful to Lakshmi Menon, my English teacher, who taught me how to appreciate the language: through her fun stories, calculated feeds of CBSE textbook formula, and superhuman levels of patience. And finally, I would like to embrace my well-wishers, weep into their ears, and tell them that I would still be fixing ACs and playing it safe till the day I die if not for their encouragement. Thank you.

Miss Valentine

A daughter was born to a count and
his wife, Valentine.
To their surprise, Valentine,
named after her mother;
That being all they had in similar,
was born with a mango shaped head,
white eyes,
and a smile most dire a sight:
looking like a garland of many teeth woven and
worn by a proud hunter of mice.

The countess bit her scream,
delayed a faint induced by this
grotesque thing.

Hopefully, with thorough inspection
something of theirs they hoped to see…

But,

neither of them had clouded eyes.
"Is she the daughter of a fish on ice?
or is she blind?!" thought the mother.
Alarmed by the latter thought,
she waved at young Valentine, and

thankfully,
the little one smiled,
and chuckled at them
in the sound of cricket's cry.

Though, it had taken an entire
fortnight,
the parents were ready…
to love, and to lie.

Charting Antarctica

"Forgive us! Spare us, oh mother of heaven!"
The shivering monks spoke up.
Thinking their watchful Lord had slept.
They begged to clear blue sky,
shouting chants, while in inner shouted vile.
A wedge of ice flinched and made the boards cry,
thereby waking me.
I said to me, "Forgive me, Mother mine,
for I might never return."

Below deck, I went coughing.
The cold woke the vengeance of past smoked tob.
The inside, where water had sprayed through bleeding hull,
was now, to my surprise,
crystalline.

A fair tooth of this vulgar land had lodged inside her.
It had pierced her back a while.
Now she, St. Jeremy's grace,
Lay half sunk and frozen.

Comical was the thought of St. Jeremy's face.
If he could see her now.
Wrecked, mid holy crusade;
his ship lay with a belly filled of ice.

The monks will see their god first, if they sit and pray.

Spectres of ice twirled 'tween footing,
And circling, hugging my charts.
Charts, that were prior floating,
now, frozen where they lay.

Only the mountain gods reside here,
Along with gods of this hellish white spray.
Is this Hell, of which I was kept afraid?
My stones are freezing.
Where the devil is that hell fire they say?

I ripped the charts from ice's maw.
The ice was strong, though froze moments ago.
Then, climbed deckward and flung a gaze to her side
and saw St. Jeremy clamped 'tween massive jaws.
Then, with my charts, overboard:
Onto lands lonelier than any sea,
The loneliest I ever saw.
I, alone, began walking the life out of me.

My water, ice; the oil in my rations had frozen it to a block,
till all I had was a burden, a bag full of rocks.

Charting and walking these godforsaken lands,
"Civilization be damned for sending me,"
I shouted to the mountains,
and the ice under my toes.

Buffaloman

A foreigner who filled his days at the slaughter shed,
Leaned against the faucet;
Studying the moon,
squeezing a black, lathery pool of beef blood and dish soap.
A moment's glimpse at the draining whirl told him everything.
He lived alone by the nets, amid cats and discarded fish heads.

He once collected sardine eyes in a jar for amusement:
Beautiful at first,
But later, by time, became a jar of dirty red.

A short swim in the cold moonlit river,
from bank to mid-width biting a bottle,
And he could bottle water that didn't taste of fish;
Better than the bottled kind sold for a few pretty pennies.
But the whirl said onto he, "Fish and water isn't plenty…"
There was enough to keep him living as the new helper at the shed.
"But why leave home, if only to settle at another dead end?"
The thought came and never went.
He watched the moon with intent.

A week later, around blooming night,
four men left their huts;
Each left their homes with their faces wrapped in towels.

Only one had returned.

"The others are with the Buffaloman, who found us at the bridge.
We found him, staring, standing still on his stilted buffalo legs."
And at the bridge, True to the ramblings, they had found three bodies:
a great big buffalo mess.
Not a bruise on them; not a bump; it was fright that had snuffed them.
Fright was the only evidence in frozen expression on their dead open-maw heads.

The town was robbed of their three lovable vagabonds;
The vagabonds, of their wallets;
And the butcher, of his helper, a rotting buffalo head from the pile,
And two skinned buffalo legs.

The Eldertree of Dwyt

If a babe goes missing in Dwyt,
The mimicking trees wake,
playfully
bellowing in chorus of its familiar cry.

Weigh your worth against that of the lost.
When Sol looks away,
dishonest trees passionately lie.
In Dwyt,
never you enter the woods at night.

I've seen it. I've felt it. I've smelt it. I still fear it...

the Eldertree...

I remember clearly,
it gliding along soft bog round where I lay
Paralyzed;
Rowing through the soft muck with legs of log and bearded toes.

Even now that terrible man-oak visits my sleep,
That Eldertree,

through a hewn maw in its trunk calling, "Mummy!

Mummy!"
Calling in my voice, it was terribly uncanny.

That behemoth,

It slithered in circles,
frenzied for my mother's flesh
but, she never came.
Thankfully...

She waited for me,
Loving mother. Mummy...
scant of meal and sleep,
She hugged me
when I came with the freedom I bought from it,
From the Eldertree.
At that time, the fee didn't at all matter to me.

She hugged me,
and tied a shawl around my spewing malady
when I came one-armed and crying.

The tree wears it now on its right:
my supple skin and my father's ring.

And when it is cold,
the pain mocks me.
When sleep evades the sting of that old mark of barter,
my wound,
I'm reminded through sublime flashes:
of its fleshy face, stolen from some poor soul

undoubtedly...
Impaled,
puppeteered by protruding wooden scales underneath
Like a banner of a smile
with squinted merry eyes.
I see it in my dreams:
It smiling silently;
expecting, but not asking for the rest of I.

I was eighteen when it took me, now I'm twenty-three.
The town had progressed,
but my shame-cast phantom limb reminded me of he,
that sickly Eldertree.
A thing of the green awaiting flesh, mine, to wear?
My skin to feel? My tongue to taste? My stones to breed?

"It of bark, of moss, and human rot!
I've come for you at last!
I and mine axe!"
I took a swig of something strong.
So my hands would clutch;
so I, be as can be, relaxed.

I entered the bog... older, stronger...

And there it stood, that bastardly oak.
The old face it wore now decomposed,
now a black canvas of rot...
but still bearing that crescent smile,
Its branches hung high, ready to hug me tight.
And...

         my old arm,
      with a skin of mould,
         taunting me
with own wiggling dead fingers of mine...

Bagef Kox

I once shared a room with a Bagef Kox the second.
Though he'd never told me where he was from,
I knew it was obviously the pet shop.
Where else are hamsters from?
I was the snake in the case, of course.

I just sat there, on two-thirds of my coiled self,
Smiling all day;
Mocking silently his spouts of fright:
Rooted from plastic whenever he went forwards or back.
He was too simple to know left or right.

He was put in a see-through cube
Instead of a ball, the hamster usual.
This was after days of Master's wheezing and panting;
Chasing Kox,
While Kox, was playing the dog.
His box still smelt like a Bagef Kox.
Not the second of now,
But the first;
the one before him.

Whenever in a weird mood,
I used to taunt that poor fool till he got put in the box.

"I'm a dog," said the first Bagef Kox to me, finally,
after I'd convinced him that the dog was hoarding all the
love.

He started wagging his stubby tail and drooling.
And for running around, Kox was put in a box.
Relentlessly, he went with the routine! He kept it up!
Till they figured he was ill.

That was the end of Master's playmate.
Poor he,
Fed to the snake in the case.

Hunger

A queer looking fellow had flung a bucket
where their me they kept.
In throw, half the water wet the floor,
And the remainder swayed and wept.
And I, a cobbler, human foremost,
thirsty,
suckled the ground like a teat.

The sky is where he's known to reside.
So, through my window, afternoons long I cried.
Then by evening, on the floor I lay, deflated and petrified
wondering, "With so many children,
How could He decide?"
Silly, skinny me, in the corner I shied.
Just I and the ammoniacal air,
and its foul taste on tongue
That I could associate and tolerate,
knowing the rancid stench of budget wine.
The kind that sped me here.
The more I drank,
the more I felt addicted to petty crimes.

And one day, he'd arrived:
A queerer looking fellow wearing a wig.
My eye latched onto his belly.

For days I could thrive on that man-pig.
wonderstruck by the sight of the swine's clothes:
Like a child would paint a plump silhouette,
coloured unimaginably.

I stared at it as I wet my throat.
The belly was the sound of a dinnerbell as sight,
To the dog called I.

"How would I cook you?"
"Loof yrgnuh siht ta kool! HAHAHAHA."
He flung words that meant nothing.

Then, till I'd dozed, I watched him.

He woke me with his laughter.
I'd found him standing in his ration of moon-shine,
shedding his fat: little by little to entire;
untying the many knots hidden under his attire.

Finally, he was slender.
Any buzzard would moan at the way he was in the
moonlight:
A fat man prior moon-shone,
now perfectly glued bones.

He crossed over to the adjacent cell on the left side: mine.
After slipping through the bars,
he's squatted
and lifted my fatter limbs and said,
"No go far."

Then he slid away.

To my side,
The dropped sacks of fat were that of a cow.
Beef! Cooked medium rare and left mildly bloody.
My mouth watered at its delicious red.
I reached, pulled and attacked the body-warmed, cooked flesh.
The flesh was sweet, salty and perfect.

Narcissist

A narcissist of a man spends his days fishing praise on
Instagram.
Crumpled are his hours so simply in page.
All members of the bin, great,
but each sensibly deemed a waste.
From them, the many botched ideas in the bin's within,
dripped the excess of his painfully preserved rage.
He had set out for the business of selling his pain,
But no one would buy.

He squeezed and drank from them every drop of passion
that came.
He ate from his gone hours spent painting vague.
He had eaten so much that he was starving.

He then abandoned the page and penned on the perfect
walls
while butterflies in gut fluttered atop ulcers.
In his mind, in his belly's within,
Like snakes they crawled.

He scratched, and scratched at that perfect paint,
His flesh begged him to stop,
His flesh hummed with pain, but he was under a spell of

Envy.

A strange thought came, Frustration made:
Saying inanimate it was more perfect than he;
More than he could ever yearn to be.
So, more angrily,
He scratched, and scratched
Till he had half-detached a fingernail.
He then quickly ripped it off.

He was desperate for workable pain.
"I'll be better than all, or die of effort and shame."
Secretly, the mastery he always felt within nudged at his defeated brain.
On the wall was a love letter in claw marks and the red paint of his veins;
written in blood red on perfect plastered scape.

Tears against sight, he began to shake.
Concocting still:
a masterpiece formed in his throbbing mind.
Tongue bit, nose epileptic, eyes blind;
Clutching bleeding fingers, while in series,
A hundred times he died.

"Yes!"

Blinkworld

Living an undying bedlam in his mind,
a broken mind's resident panting flesh lay sprawled on gaol's stone:
glazed in cold rain, both he and the floor.
Isolation, here's, and lightning's bright premature excitement
for its trailing shattering score,
made him sweat in the cold miraculously like alchemy, and
troubled him even the more.
The reek of old ghosts poured from claw marks:
cast shadows, written in broken mind across the interior of
the hollow stone confine.
It spewed from markings on the walls made by mad men of old.
This is an asylum after all.

Shielding his round ears,
he shot off from flesh and bone, onto a land or sea unknown:
a scantly ventured abode;
a realm of rhythmically torn,
seen and ignored between seemingly continuous sight:
rooted in the prolonged blink… so, Blinkworld.

At first, nothing…
Everywhere to go was the right and equally the wrong;

A mighty black bog it seemed from the wet on his feet,
It smelled like his own terrible reek so, felt like home.
Rising from a paralytic dull wake made of bars and stone,
His pupils bloomed wide, basking in unfathomable awe
behind lid's blindfolds:
his sight latched onto the secret of the blink.

To his fore, a pit of red: a stew of wings and tufts of chord.
It, The pit, spoke to him in the unison screams of winged
beasts,
shearing scales as they wrestled and mixed
midst chops of stray flesh spewing ebony mist
which spewed and filled till he was nowhere at all,
till it tricked him into thinking that he could step forth and
not fall.

He fell.
He was lost.

Coal miner

A humanoid-volcano, spent,
Past fearsome roars and subdued by hopeless: a distant cousin of solace.
He lay silent and seemingly dead with coal and sooty grit protruding from his flesh.
Lo and behold! Another misery-made silent wretch, tiredly fidgety for, and drooling against the apparent monolith, the double-door leading to death.
Not a window for light to taunt, not the faintest sound at earshot, so imagination devoured him into the deepest of human-taught despairs:
Wishful, tangible contrast.
Nothing contrasts easily with something, in a plight wherein nothing was no meagre holding in compare…if weighed, nothing could be seen, so tangibly, nothing was all he had.
Like a tired volcano post-terror, he laid panting; painted obsidian by the tunnel's collapse; marked by the black of forevermore ensnared;
Well-blent with thick shadows bled by the walls of its black gullet, bleeding…

Fate's Little Game

Fate is a drunk.
It clumsily struts to work, holding tight its motivations and lunch.
At its desk, fate fights for sobriety, mixing and matching tired names.
Fate, a thirteen-year-old drunk writes the shortest and most incoherent of essays,
With mistakes tethered to each of its masterworks,
For them to embrace or ache about while under the sun;
their permanent residence once displaced from the nothing they are from,
to the vast all at once without signs or say.
Fate watches their struggle to make hay:
their scramble for escape, fame, their struggles to self-sustain.
Fate is a drunken mistake:
shared equally amongst a pair, a woman and man.
Out of the fissure and into the fray comes the mistake,
crying, bloody and afraid,
Oblivious, untaught, squirming, rosy cheeked in drunk fate's image.
For fate, it is always a Saturday.
Between essays, it lays back to relax.
Fate does not take breaks, it celebrates,
it sears its children with the spite that escapes its boozy cage.

It drinks till everything spins, watching well-read parents
rope their kids,
and brand them with ready destinies and old dreams:
unearthed with pride from their withered graves.
After all, can anything be more worthy of embrace
Than that golden to someone who looks the same?
Working through the headache, this is Fate's every day.
The outrage spills onto its essays.
Hateful things write hateful things.
The ropes are taut so children can be taught to walk before
it is too late.
How can late walkers compete with the other progenies of
fate?
There is no prize because there is no winning,
for every prodigy there is, exists a squirming red mass eager
to maim,
erase,
and replace.

Insanity

Limbed he, epitome of pointlessly,
Walking to negative infinity through past steps;
through past wheres.
Arms buckled, like swords at peace,
under fabric's snare.
Waddling, straight-spined and jacketed;
footing along a locus,
moving at quantized timed advancing foot-slaps;
along one minute circles, counter clockwise,
and countlessly elapsed.

A celestial penguin is he!
Sounding majestic penguin cries;
he, in a cubicle of ice.
Redder, became the locus marked,
thicker with still-spilling blood on his every passing by.

"A thousand more to go," said his broken mind,
And he would reach coming here's before.
He doubts if he would spare his wife and child.
(Him — through initiated dead.)
He hated them.

He, whose skin and its, his uniform compact world's,
Matched; coloured as cartoon ice.

Leaning on padded walls plush and white,
when exhausted time to time.
Like a catalyst, his boredom spoke in a kind of Latin
to his sedated, stoned mind.
It twined around his mind at the speed of quickened
creeper's climb.
Like a terrible crossfade it spun.
He felt a pull, vertigo stung.
Sedated he, a lone planetoid penguin, orbiting nothing.

Once,
there was a scrape like a violin note by an amateur.
It sounded from his cell's polar door.
His lazy mind peered with one eye,
and two eyes peered back from a foreign world;
that forgot at Door's behind.
He caught them!
(With only sight; with only the stare of his eyes.)

A neon fluid cruelty danced between them,
Flowing from the yoke of his eyes, onto the white:
In no particular order he could sight.

"I forget to blink sometimes," he said, then laughed.
"The mistake is mine," he said to the eyes.
Then, again a scraping slide.
The white hatch slid shut, bridging 'tween with blind,
melting away thoughts of the outside and of the eyes from
his mind;
retiring him to is.
He has been smiling since,
For no reason known to I, nor him.

Oceans Deep

The journey is from here to the blackest deep;
from chewing soft pastes and being bathed
to fighting viciously for meals.
Oh crater scant of belly touching the back of my spine,
Oh cramped twisted feet, help me bore into this new unknown,
to find the extraordinary in a place well-guarded against pillage and empty...
(Splash, gush, and down into the deep.)

Time patiently remained company while I and the air in my lungs,
the remnant of confident entry,
both, it and me, held by the throat; both incapable of speech,
bored sporadically
to find... something... in a place told to be well-guarded against pillage and empty...
(Silence.)

Light, all at once, went away in a single arm sweep.
There was little to see for thoughts to be picky.
Foresight has always been a luxury. Such is life:
Its sustenance, to me, always a herculean feat.

I was reminded of that why as old as eternity.
I told the class what I'd be.
"An astronaut," said me, prior actuality.
When I was young, that meant swimming in space.

But when I was finally, after a long lead, out of the factory,
I hung from ceilings, fixing ACs in exchange for poverty:
earth bound, in buildings tall
and in the nights, empty.
And always in the nights, from the partially finished,
unfurnished office floors,
at hours ungodly,
I would stand in the breeze that flirted with the monolith's
highest accessible balcony…
…Dreaming of oceans deep:
Its cold entrails, its aesthetic violent, foaming, roaring
hostility.

I'm finally in the nowhere I want to be.

I must keep swimming.